# LIFE WITH WINGS

## STORY

NAFAY BAKSH

ISBN 979-888521877-1

# Contents

# Preface

*When somebody faces any problem in their life , they feel that a life as an animal is easier than a life of a human.I have heard many people talking about this situation and seen many who think that the life of an animal is very easy.Animals just eat,play,talk and sleep but humans study,work,eat and sleep."Life of an animal is very easy"this following statement if not true.The life of an animal is also very difficult.We humans make their life difficult by hunting them,by cutting the trees on which many animals live,by captureing them between the cages of iron bars and many more.These all we do to fulfill our greedy heart but animals make our life easier by providing us food such as eggs,milk,meat and many more but the most important thing that they do not only for us but for all the living organisums is that they make a balance on the planet on which we live.Now read the story to undestand how a life of a dove is.*

# Life With Wings

*I am a snowy dove and I am born in a cage.I have never visited the world outside a cage.I stay in a bird shop and Mr.Fleming lister owned the shop.He was a small fussy man with tight melon like stomach.Large glasses magnified his eyes so as to give him the appearence of a wise and genial owl.There were many birds in the shop.The other birds told me about the blue sky.*

I wondered "what is a blue sky?"where is it located?"how does it look like?"After many days the time for christmas arrived.The shop was ornated very well.then any consumer materialized in the shop,all the birds start twittering.We think that when we twitter the consumer comes and buys us and then give us the freedom which we need.One day when I was feeling monotonous,I pervaded my wings and started mopping them with my beak.Just then a customer entered the shop.He looked magnanimous.His suit was cheep,ill fitting but new.He had a shuttling glance and close cropped hair.Ignoring Fleming for a moment,he rolled his gaze around the shadowy shop.The man stared closely at Mr.Fleming as though just now aware of his presence.He said,"I wanted something with wings,which loves to fly".Mr Fleming was bewildered.Then the stranger pointed his fingure on me.I became perple.Mr.Fleming hunched down my cage and handed over to the stranger.The stranger steped out of the shop and opeaned the cage.As the cage opeaned,I flew out of the cage.Seeing this M.r felming felt vaguely insulted.I came very far from the shop.I didn't undestand how to thank that man.I started flying very high.I saw the blue land above me which looked endless.I asked myself is this the blue sky?I was very happy.Just then another bird attacked me from the back.

Before I could undestand that it was an eagle,it attacked me on my wings.However I managed to escape but I started falling down on the ground.I was not able to fly and so fall on the ground.Before closing my eyes I saw a human running towards me.When I opeaned my eyes I found myself in a pet shop but there was no fleming.I noticed that somebody kept bandage on my wings.Then a customer entered the shop.He brought two childern with him.The children were tottering in the shop.There was a long convasation between the shopkepper and the customer.After the convasation was finished the customer *pointed the fingure at me.The shopkepper unhooked my cage and handed over to them.I was glad,I thought that they are going to give me the freedom.They took me to a enormus house which looked like a grand palace.I thought that my gateway to the freedom is very close but insted of letting me free they took me to a huge cage which was made up of gold and silver.*

*The cage was so big that more than twenty birds can linger very easily.The children came near the cage and slinked around the cage.Their father briefed them to take good care of me.They always offered me luscious food in a golden cup.There was a small tree inside the cage.I would happily perch from one branch to another.Many days passed on and now I was feeling bored in the huge cage.There was no other bird to talk with.No one was taking care of me properly and so I was feeling gaunt.The whole family went for a picnic trip to enjoy their holidays.I was starving.I slinked from one branch to another in search of food.More than food I was striving for my freedom.My hunger was*

*going to make me frantic and frenzied.I waited the whole day for them to return and offer me food.At the end I lost my patience and thought that I have got my freedom forever.*

# Moral

*I hope the reader undestad that life for everyone is equal.Neither difficult nor easy But the most important thing is that there should be nothing inequal because inequality will end the huminity.So end inequality before inequality ends the huminity.*

thank you for spending your time to read this book.

Enter Caption